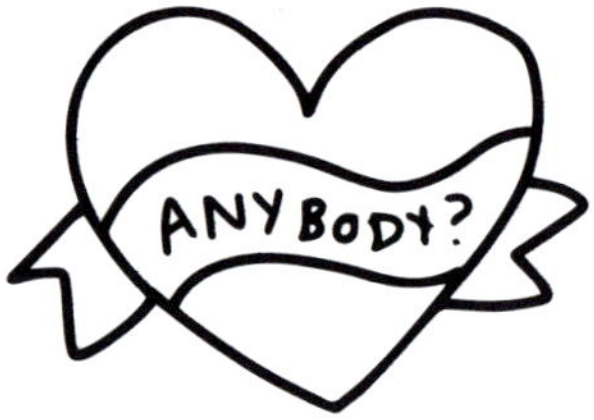
ANYBODY?

But Like Maybe Don't?

ARIANNA MARGULIS

But Like Maybe Don't?

What Not to Do When Dating

AN ILLUSTRATED GUIDE

RODALE.
New York

Published in the United States by Rodale Books,
an imprint of Random House, a division of Penguin Random House LLC, New York.

rodalebooks.com

Rodale Books is a registered trademark,
and the Circle colophon is a trademark of
Penguin Random House LLC.

Some of the drawings in this work originally
appeared on the author's Instagram.

Library of Congress
Cataloging-in-Publication Data is
available upon request.

ISBN 978-0-593-13660-7
Ebook ISBN 978-0-593-13661-4

Printed and bound in Italy by L.E.G.O. S.p.A.

Book and Cover Illustrations by Arianna Margulis
Book and Cover design by Francesca Truman

10 9 8 7 6 5 4 3 2 1

First Edition

This book is
dedicated to all of my

"ex-boyfriends."

I HOPE YOU'RE SORRY
NOW THAT I'M A FANCY
PUBLISHED AUTHOR.

Foreword

Have you ever looked up at the sky after having your heart smooshed and thought, **What is wrong with me?!**

More times than you can count? Because LOL, same.

Let me first begin by saying that NOTHING is wrong with you. You're a gosh darn unicorn. Glitter runs through your veins. But you could be doing some stuff that's wrong. Like I did.

My name is Arianna Margulis and I'm a *reformed* serial dater. All of my many, many "relationships" from high school through about age thirty topped out at three months. My sweet spot was around three weeks. My friends like to joke that I've been on a date with every guy in Manhattan, and I gently remind them—don't forget most of Brooklyn, too. How had I NEVER had a serious boyfriend? I always fell so hard, and too fast. I had no problem finding guys I liked, I just had problems keeping them around. I never understood it.

¯_(ツ)_/¯

But, somehow, I remained ever hopeful. I always thought, **The next guy I meet could be my husband!**

Growing up in a small town in Michigan, that's how I thought it was supposed to work. Meet someone in college, get married, have babies. Why was it taking me so gosh dang long?

Now, for the first time, I can say I know what love feels like. (Reciprocated love.) It prompted me to think, *What was different this time?* And I realized the difference was me. Looking back, I truly believe that I reeked of insecurity and desperation. I brainwashed myself into believing that I needed to catch up with some timeline and constantly compared my romantic relationships to others around me.

I was obsessed with the idea of love. So obsessed with the thought that my happiness lay with finding a man. I used to think, *If I just get a boyfriend, I'll finally be happy*. Life would fall into place. I was fixated on finding someone and ignored everything else, especially myself. I admittedly had no serious personal goals, dreams, or aspirations besides "him." I couldn't discover or love me because I was too busy trying to find someone else to love.

Let me take you back to one of my breakthrough moments

(WHIMSICAL FLASHBACK MUSIC . . .)

It was a gorgeous day at the tail end of May in New York City. The Tuesday after Memorial Day, to be exact. Why do I remember this? Well, I had just returned after a magical weekend with my then-"boyfriend." Let's call him . . . Cooper, which is obviously not his real name.

Cooper's family lived in Maine, some adorable town with a strip of stores that look like cottages, a town where everyone knew one another by name. We had only been seeing each other a couple of months, but it had escalated quickly. I had never really met anyone's parents before. I was on a cloud when I came back to the city because the report was in: his mom, dad, cousins, everyone loved me!

Cooper had texted me that afternoon to meet him outside of his office on Fifth Avenue. We would go for a walk in Central Park. Swoon, how perfect.

We held hands as we strolled but didn't get very far when he asked to sit down on a park bench. He put his hand on my thigh. He looked at me. Was he going to tell me he loved me? Was this it? Was I finally going to hear the words with meaning for the very first time?

He began, "I just want to say, you're an amazing girl, but—"

And there it was. My heart sank. Those words I had heard so many times before, and I knew what was to follow. This wasn't a declaration of love. It was a good old-fashioned dumping.

He went on to tell me that he wasn't himself anymore, he needed to focus on work, and I had really thrown off his meditation schedule. That was the line that made me want to burst out laughing and crying at the very same time. I repeat, *I threw off his meditation schedule*. I ripped his hand off my thigh and told him that I never wanted to speak to him again. And I didn't—until a year or so later, when I found myself drunkenly yelling at him at a night club circa 3 A.M. But more on that later. I walked to Fifth Avenue and dramatically screamed, "TAXI!!!," leaving him in the dust. (I'd always wanted to do that anyway.)

I could still show you the exact park bench where it happened.

I celebrate this story because, for the first time, I didn't wallow. I laughed, and I used the breakup (sorry, okay, dumping) as fuel. I threw myself into a creative venture. I started doodling all sorts of funny breakup toons. I started reflecting on all of the stories that came before. The pain of the past was beginning to turn into pleasure. It was an epiphany!

The irony is, by sharing my insecurities and horror stories, I was able to laugh at myself. I started to enjoy my journey and all the frogs I kissed. Or, all the frogs that went leaping away from me. I was creating something from pain, something I valued way more than a boyfriend. I was making something that I was proud of and sharing it with the world. I turned my broken heart into art. I learned to love me first (*cheese alert*), which I believe is the key to loving someone else.

Oh man, did it take A LOT to get me to this point.

As you continue to read, you'll see that I have no business writing a dating guide. Nothing I did ever worked. I have no hot tips on how to reel him in. I have no secret potions or spells. (Wouldn't that be nice?) What I can offer you, though, is where I went wrong. Where I went *oh-so-very-embarrassingly, wow-really-tho?* wrong. I have stories. Lots and lots of stories. **No dos, just don'ts.**

I kind of think that's what I discovered. There's no reeling anyone in. There's no trickery. There's just you, being yourself. Someone will see you doing your thang and say to himself or herself or their gender-non-binary self, "I want to be a part of their world." Where we go wrong is when we don't trust that that's even possible, so we start trying to make it happen. You get a PhD in emojis and read receipts. You ascribe magical powers to certain tops and lip glosses. You pretend to be really into rock climbing despite your crippling fear of heights. This book is about helping you to COOL IT.

And a note about gender. Since I'm a woman who dates men, my stories are from that perspective, but dating is dating, and love is love. I think these are some pretty universal experiences. Whoever you are and whomever you love, this book is for you. Girls who date girls also do the seductive slow fade, boys who date boys also sometimes move across the country to surprise a summer fling (LOLZ, more on that later), and everything in between. Stop chasing, get reading, and start loving on YOU. I want you to enjoy and learn from my mistakes. I want you to laugh, cringe, and relate to them.

AND THEN
I WANT YOU NEVER TO DO THEM AGAIN,
OKAY???????

Let's start at the beginning.

Remember being a kid and thinking:

Or as you got a little older . . .

How many of you have done this?

My poor parents. They stopped getting excited after the twenty-seventh time I said that. We all had expectations like this when we were young. But you know what they say about when you assume . . .

You make an ASS out of you and—well, you.

So if this is looking a little
too familiar and, whoopsie,

Get some expectations more in line with this:

WEEK 1: BUTTERFLIES

WEEK 2: TEXTS BECOME SPARSE

WEEK 3: HE DISAPPEARS INTO THE ABYSS

AW, JUST KIDDING. Well, sort of.

Please analyze this highly scientific chart, and do your best to make it to the top. SETTLE FOR NOTHING LESS.

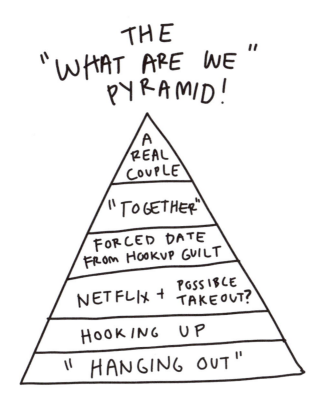

THE "WHAT ARE WE" PYRAMID!

A REAL COUPLE

"TOGETHER"

FORCED DATE FROM HOOKUP GUILT

NETFLIX + POSSIBLE TAKEOUT?

HOOKING UP

"HANGING OUT"

Basically, if you're anywhere but at the top of this chart, run. "Together" is just a thing we made up to make ourselves feel better. IT'S NOT REAL. And if you have to ask "what are we"—if you even have to wonder—ALSO RUN.

Did you get all that?

Okay, cool. Now prepare yourself for all the bottom-feeding I did and pay attention to what not to do.

Table of No-Nos

Luring Them In
What Won't Work (TRUST ME)

27

Desperate Debbie
Calm the Crazy

49

When They Disappear
Face the Harsh Reality

85

Don't Go Back!

Just Don't

113

Boy Bye

You Didn't Really Like Them Anyway

139

Focusing on You

I Mean, You Get This One, Right?

161

Acknowledgments

175

Luring Them In

What Won't Work

(TRUST ME)

We can sometimes let our poor judgment get the best of us when we meet someone new. Let me take you back to high school and my very first time. (Sorry, Dad.)

This may be the mistake that started it all.

I was a teen in high school just starting to find myself. I was a bit of a late bloomer, not traditionally "cool" or "popular" but instead fading into the artsy middle space. But things were finally starting to turn. I had just gotten my first round of highlights and started wearing a padded bra. I got a job at Hollister at the mall, so skimpy clothes came in on discount. I had given up on boys at my own school, but I started meeting friends at neighboring high schools, where I had a clean slate. For all they knew, I was the coolest girl in my class.

My rival high school had the best lacrosse team in the state—and the cutest guys. In Michigan, lacrosse was our *Friday Night Lights*. Spotlight on Liam. He had a scholarship to play the following year at college on the East Coast. He was handsome, drove a fast car, and wore Jean Paul Gaultier cologne that still stops me today when I smell it on a passerby. He had a hot, cool mom and tons of rowdy jock friends. He was a bad boy with a Colgate smile. **I wanted him.**

I put the word out through friends that I was interested. I was going to find a way to be his number-wearing, sideline-cheering girlfriend.

One evening, my friend's parents were out of town, and we threw a Solo cup basement high school party. Liam and I had been texting a lot and had even hung out a few times in groups. He took me to a hockey game (he had season tickets) and even dinner at the mall. We went to J. Alexander's, which was our town's newest chain restaurant—very see and be seen.

Party time came, and he arrived with some friends and a bottle of some fruity liquor I liked. We talked about lacrosse, finals, prom. It was all happening. I couldn't believe that someone of this social magnitude was paying attention to ME. How jealous would everyone be, I wondered. *Who is this girl?*, they would think. We were canoodling all night, and my friend, the hostess, had told me she would lend me her bedroom for the evening. **I had prepared myself for this to be THE night.**

I had never had sex before. To be frank, it was awkward AF. I had no idea what I was doing. I told him it was my first time, and he tried to make me comfortable. I used some sort of Bath & Body Works lotion to get things going. Probably had sparkles in it. And we did it. Was this it? Was this what everyone talked about? I definitely didn't orgasm, but I pretended I did because I heard that's what you do. Afterward, I couldn't sleep all night. He did. I just kinda lay there, excited about us and what was next.

By the time the sun came up, Snow White's birds began chirping around my head. I remember waiting for his eyes to open for what seemed like forever. I rustled around in the covers, hoping to wake him. Now that we did it, we were official, right?!

From the moment he woke up, though, he was distant. I tried to cuddle, and he just wanted to get out of there. It was nothing like the night before. Prom and his number sweatshirt started to collapse in my dreams. I was scared. I had to secure the relationship and my place somehow. So I asked to see his phone. I went to my contact and changed my name to . . .

Yep. I changed my name in his phone to Princess.

Oh wait, no, sorry:

~*pRiNcEsS*~

I texted him later that day to see if he wanted to get ice cream. That's what couples do, right? Well, guess what? He didn't text Princess back. Did not call, did not visit, did not ever respond again.

Some people laugh when I tell this story and try to comfort me by saying, "Well, maybe he just couldn't find you in his phone!"

I wasn't hard to find. In his phone or IRL. I would leave incessant messages. I drove through his neighborhood and near his school around dismissal. I even convinced my friends to take me to hockey playoff games in the hopes of running into him. If I saw the same make of his car on the street, my heart would drop, and I'd follow it for a while, only to realize it was just another black Jeep that a suburban mom was driving. I remember not understanding. This wasn't how it was supposed to go.

Eventually I found out he got back together with his ex-girlfriend, who was a tennis star. You'd think that'd be the end of it, but no—I joined my school's team, hoping to face off against her. I befriended a girl out of nowhere because I knew she babysat his little sister. Anything to get close to him. He was able to successfully avoid me. So you can comfort me all you want, but we all know the truth. **Princess spooked the crap out of him.**

What else can you do to scare someone too early besides nicknaming yourself Princess? Well, you could use my standard first date question, "What kind of wedding cake do you think you want?" Oh wow, I know. For some reason, I thought it was charming. And I thought it would also clue me in to if they were ready for marriage . . .

Oh, this was a fun one: Once I remember asking a guy I had only been on a few dates with if we would raise our kids with Christianity, Judaism, or both.

This was also another one of my favorite things to mention too early:

Besides scaring him IRL, be sure to not freak him out with all things internet. **Stalking his social media in the early stages is important, but you must remember to keep your cool.** You can't let on that you knew his cousin got married in Spain last September.

You can also find out things about a person you wish you didn't. One spring night in my mid-twenties, my room-mate, Allison, and I decided to hit a swanky club. We started flirting with this table of guys who were celebrating a graduation. I took a shine to the man of the hour, and we danced all night, made out, you know the drill. I remember waking up the next day and showing Allison the rose he had bought me from a guy outside the club. I said I was in love. "Let's look him up!" she said.

We found Charles Charlesington IV on Facebook and read that he attended the Ken Kensington School. "I've never heard of that college, sounds fancy—maybe it's in London?" We quickly realized that we had not attended his grad school or college graduation festivities the night before. Ken Kensington was a New York City high school. **I had been making out all night with a very mature seventeen-year-old.**

Another stalking gone particularly wrong occurred after a friend found what seemed to be a very incriminating photo of a guy, Miles, I was seeing while home one summer from college. In said photo, Miles was snuggled up with another girl, and they were both wearing University of Michigan jerseys. The caption read, "Can't wait until next year!" I was furious. In a blind rage, I went to his apartment. His roommate let me in but said that Miles wasn't home. I ran upstairs to his room and threw open

PROS

YOU FIND HIS EX

YOU FIND HIS BROTHER

YOU FIND OUT WHERE HE LIVES

YOU FIND PICS OF HIS DOG

CONS

SHE'S CUTE

YOU SLEPT WITH HIM

YOU SHOW UP THERE DRUNK

YOU LIKE THE DOG MORE THAN HIM

the drawer where he kept the lube we would use. A fresh bottle, perfect. I ripped off the cap and sprayed the entire room, drenching his sheets, drapes, EVERYTHING in slippery sex gel. I took a framed picture of us I had given him and smashed it on the ground. Shards of glass everywhere. I walked downstairs, thanked his cackling roommate, and left. Hours later, I would come to find out Miles had a younger, attractive, female cousin, who found out she was going to be attending the University of Michigan in the fall.

And, most important, stay away from his ex's page. Okay, who am I kidding, just be careful, all right? Keep your invisibility cloak on and stay away from Stories. Anything that leaves a footprint.

I, for one, have a stalking account.

Her name is Tiffany, and she goes to Florida State.

And make sure your friends
are careful, too.

Wouldn't it be nice if this existed to school us all?

Be yourself. Don't pretend to like his favorite band. Don't pretend to like ice cream if dairy gives you gas. Trust me on this one, guys—it won't end well.

One of these days the lies will catch up with you. Like in *Clueless*, when Cher thought Billie Holiday was a dude.

And don't make grand gestures too early in the game. I liked to use arts and crafts to lure men in. It was kind of my signature move. Wouldn't they find a handmade card of construction paper and Elmer's glue from a twenty-something woman adorable? One Valentine's Day, I was hooking up with a very talented, world-renowned artist. I thought that showing off my creativity with a life-size paper heart would surely make him think us "artists" were meant to be together. I stayed up all night glue-gunning and sparkling. Pom-pomming and lacing. I cut photos from magazines and art books to add a collage-like effect. I didn't want it to seem basic. This was a hipster valentine. I texted him and told him I had something to present to him for the special day, one artist to another. No answer. I couldn't let my hard work go to waste!

I made a little video of me holding the masterpiece, blowing a kiss to the camera. I texted it to him. No reply. Maybe something was just wrong with his phone?! In a final move of desperation, I went to his apartment. He lived in a Brooklyn townhouse, so he actually had a front door. I left it on the doorstep, rang the bell, and sprinted away.

I got a pity text from him the next day. "Haha nice." He haha niced me. He haha niced my Valentine. I felt like he was my fourth-grade art teacher giving me a sad silver star. And poof! As quickly as the glue dried . . . **he was gone.**

NOBODY CHOO-CHOO CHOOSED ME

Desperate
Debbie
Calm the Crazy

Okay, so let's say you've managed to go on a few dates, and that magical swirly butterfly feeling in your tummy has arrived. **It feels like nothing else in the world.** Is this what rainbows are made of? Puppies and sunshine? It makes you want to skip in the street, dance on a desk, and tell the world you're in love, you're in love, and you don't care who knows it!!! It can also make you do some real psycho stuff.

**Let's just make sure we don't
self-sabotage, shall we?**

ANATOMY OF A FINANCE BRO

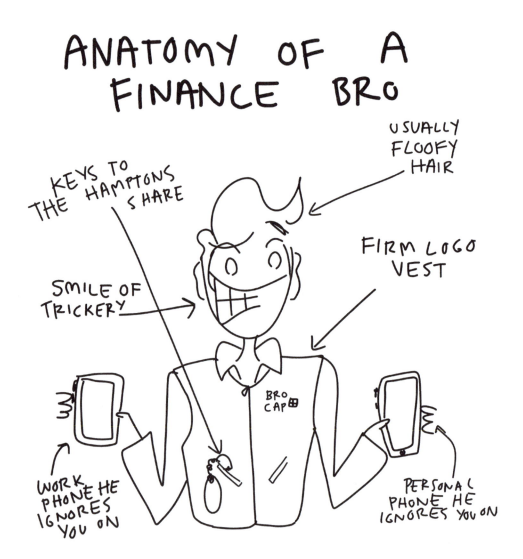

USUALLY FLOOFY HAIR

KEYS TO THE HAMPTONS SHARE

FIRM LOGO VEST

SMILE OF TRICKERY

BRO CAP

WORK PHONE HE IGNORES YOU ON

PERSONAL PHONE HE IGNORES YOU ON

One summer, I decided to join a Hamptons share house with a group of my friends in the hope of meeting someone. I had gotten pretty down after a New York City winter full of finance-bro failures.

Enter Jay, this tall, dark, and handsome friend of a friend. I met him at a Fourth of July party. We kissed for the first time under fricking fireworks. He asked how on earth I was still single. I love when guys ask that. I dunno, because I'm a relationship-obsessed psycho? Why, you down to ride?

Jay was unlike anyone I had ever dated. He shared his feelings. He wanted to do ACTIVITIES together! We rode bikes, we made picnics, we went to museums and independent film screenings. He called—like, voice calls. How had I found such an emotionally evolved man?!

Then I figured out how. In August, he decided to break the news to me. He was moving to L.A. in September. He claimed he didn't want to tell me when we first met because he thought I wouldn't like him anymore. Perhaps he was so open and free in the progression of our "relationship" because he knew it had a safe, forced end.

It's cute that he didn't realize the depth of my insanity. He thought that by telling me this, he was breaking it off, clean and simple. LOL. Unbeknownst to him, I went to my boss at Ralph Lauren and requested a transfer to

L.A. I told myself and everyone around me that this move was "for me" (eye roll). There was no way I was going to let this feeling fade—we were so obviously meant to be together! I'd follow him and force this to work. We were like Sandy and Danny, if Sandy purposefully enrolled at Rydell High and didn't tell Danny beforehand. When the time came for him to go, I told him, "GUESS WHAT! I'm moving to L.A., too!!!!!"

Jay was less than thrilled. His reaction was a mix of utter shock, fear, and a garbled, "Well, wow, see you out there soon then."

When I got to L.A., he took me to a pity movie.
A matinee.
And that was that.

I hope you enjoyed that example of an advanced crazy move, no pun intended. Okay, LOL, pun intended.

Let's focus on some more of the entry-level crazy things I used to do.

I started seeing this guy, Jordan, in high school, PP (post princess). He was creative, played guitar, artsy. It was his birthday, and Burberry plaid was in its prime, so I went to the mall with all my Hollister money and bought him the manliest thing Burberry sold—a plaid polo shirt. I presented it to him at the bus stop the next morning. I was so proud. And he actually liked it! When we parted ways at the end of the day, I asked him, "Are you going to wear it tomorrow?!" And he assured me he would. If you saw my face, I looked like the Grinch with that creepy, plotting smile.

The next morning, I put on my mom's Burberry plaid skirt.

**That's right.
We were going to match.
It would be adorable.**

Before I got to class he texted me that everyone was so impressed with his new Burberry shirt. I was so excited. I walked into our school's common area and spotted him across the room. As I got closer, he grew red.

"YOU MADE US MATCH ON PURPOSE?!"

The entire room exploded in laughter. All the guys started teasing him. I tried to say it was a coincidence, but we all knew the truth. The "Burberry story" lives on to this day among my high school friends, but, sadly, Jordan's and my story as a couple ended shortly after.

Forcing apparel is almost as bad as forcing a run-in.

Ahh, one of my favorite pastimes.

Classic. I feel so bad for my friends who I dragged around in circles. Here's the thing. If someone wants to see you, they'll make it happen. Don't go barhopping.

I can't tell you how many nights I've wasted searching for someone instead of actually having fun. There was one infamous downtown bar, Happy Endings, that I would hit at 11 P.M. and 2 A.M., checking both the early and late shifts for my man of the moment. If I did a lap and they weren't there, I would exit immediately and be off to the next place. I would consider a night ruined without some sort of male crush interaction. **I was consumed.**

And definitely don't "happen" to show up places you know he frequents. Like his house. For most, this is a "well, duh," but I found it completely acceptable at a time in my life. I once saw a guy jump when I sneak-attack brought him coffee. I thought he would find it sweet . . .

I once became obsessed with this guy, Omar, who I met at a holiday party. He didn't ask for my number at said party, and I gave him plenty of chances, but that didn't stop me. During our conversation he mentioned he worked for a major advertising firm. I looked up where the firm's office was—just an easy ten blocks from my apartment! Every day around 6 P.M. (for what was probably months) I would go out of my way ten blocks, apply lip gloss, and walk past his office verrrry slowly, hoping to run into him on his way home. It didn't ever work, by the way.

Don't set yourself up for disappointment.

Don't be a puppy.

By which I mean, don't be so available. I was once on an airplane home from New York to Detroit. I had just been told by a guy twice my age that he wasn't looking for anything serious. Pretty much the only reason I was dating the old man was because I thought he'd actually commit. You know, because his age meant he *must* be more mature. Not in New York! Peter Pan syndrome, I think they call it.

I was so bummed about the whole situation that I decided a trip home would cure me. I was ensconced in a middle seat in coach when my phone pinged. It was the old man. The text read something like, "bbq tonight at Freddy's, you in?" Well, psh, that was all I needed! A BBQ at Freddy's—hot diggity!

I deplaned the aircraft. The flight attendant told me that I would not be able to get my checked bags if I left. I didn't care. My luggage went to Detroit, and I didn't. (And, obviously, the "relationship" went nowhere.)

And a friendly reminder:

Don't drive yourself insane checking social media.
Counting minutes between texts, analyzing responses.
I mean, okay, I still do it, but I'm just trying to warn you,
it messes with your brain. It makes the crazy juice kick
into hyperdrive.

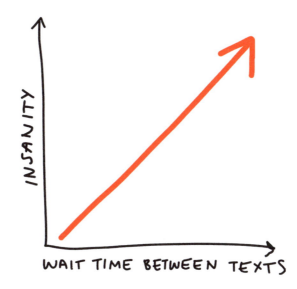

Set yourself some boundaries.

I allow myself to initiate one text convo a week.

If you do send a message,
especially on Instagram,
don't keep checking to see
if they've read it.

Instead, be pleasantly surprised when they respond. Or you can swipe to delete your message if they don't reply within a couple days. That's what I like to do. That way, you just never really know. Maybe their phone got stolen. Maybe a shark ate them.

Ignorance is bliss.

Do not,
I repeat,
DO NOT
listen to
alcohol.

I'd say about 99.9 percent of the mistakes I've made in "relationships" (why do I keep using this word?) happened when I've been under the influence. And usually way too early in the game.

Booze can be like truth serum.

And also kind of like jet fuel.

And also like Benadryl? Once I fell asleep (okay, passed out) on this guy I was seeing. He told me that I claimed I just needed a power nap and to wake me up in twenty and I'd be good to keep partying.

One night I was drunk texting with this model, Damien, who I had met on a dating app and who lived in Los Angeles. I told him I would be out there the following night for a "work trip" and I would love to see him. There was no work trip. I didn't even have a job that had work trips. Instead, I drunk bought a plane ticket on JetBlue. And what's worse is that I actually boarded the flight the next day thinking this would be a neat adventure. **He could be my husband, you never know!** I remember packing an overnight bag and Allison (who was used to my antics by now) asked where I was going. I said L.A., but I'd be back by tomorrow if she wanted to go out. I was in Los Angeles for less than twenty-four hours, and I had him pick me up at some random office building where I pretended my meetings were held.

To combat my alcohol-induced
alter ego, I have a favorite trick.

I guess I never really followed
my own rules, though.

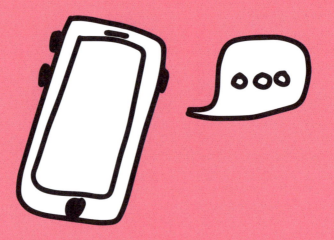

When They Disappear

Face the Harsh Reality

So the texts are getting fewer. The responses are getting shorter. I've personally never successfully recovered from a slow fade—and I'd actually love to know if anyone ever has.

It was another summer in New York, and I had met the man of my dreams.

(YES, AGAIN.)

His name was Brandon. Ivy League grad, high-level finance job, with a head of curly hair and serious dance moves. He made me feel special. He thought I was charming, adorable, quirky. I made him laugh. We were drowning in new-crush feeling. I was thrown into his world quickly, and his friends became my friends. They were all so hip, so downtown. He wasn't your average Midtown money guy. It was a scene I had never really experienced before, and it was intoxicating. Everyone around him was starting some fabulous company, or they were models, artists, writers, or pseudo–New York royalty. And he was throwing little old Midwestern me into the mix.

He would pick me up on Fridays, and we would hit the Hamptons. Chic parties and dancing all night under the stars—I got used to this lifestyle and his crew very quickly. I started to forget my own. I wouldn't ask my friends what they were up to anymore because I knew I would be spending all my time with Brandon.

One weekend, I felt it change. He picked me up on Friday, but there were two other girls in the car. One was from some fancy school in Paris, the other's family came in on the *Mayflower* or something. All of their designer luggage matched. Everything from bikinis to beauty products were luxury, coordinated. And then there I was, with my duffel bag and crusty drugstore bronzer.

I remember feeling lost in conversation. They were all chatting about friends in common, and I had less and less to contribute. They got on the topic of European vacations, and I mentioned I went to Montréal in Canada once and it was lovely. (That was the only other country I had been to at that point.) The entire weekend, I felt like the third wheel. I wasn't shiny and new. My silly energy was no longer cute. Suddenly it was childish. Brandon started to make me the butt of jokes. I would end up alone at parties and find them all in a room together somewhere, laughing.

The night before we left, I asked him, "Brandon, am I your girlfriend?" Which, by the way, **if you have to ask, you already know the answer.**

He laughed at me. And then shrugged, "We're having fun."

You know that feeling when you know it's over? But you keep on going? You try to smoosh that stupid awful pain back down into the dirt from whence it came?

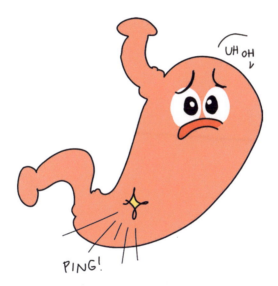

When we were back in the city that week, I didn't hear from him. I started texting him more to make plans. His texts were shorter, unenthused, and came hours after mine.

He did manage to take me out to dinner on my birthday. Probably out of guilt. I'll never forget that night. I had hope for us. I bought a new hot pink dress. It was a bit on the short side, (okay, very, very on the short side) but hey, why not, it was my day and I felt fabulous in it! I think the restaurant was called Market . . . it was somewhere in the flatiron district. When we arrived for our reservation we ran into a couple he knew. They were something out of *The Preppy Handbook*, pearls and plaids. Brandon embraced them, they chatted for what seemed like hours but probably only minutes. And there I stood behind him. Like a dummy. No introduction, no mention, nothing. I felt so stupid that I left and went to be seated alone. When he finally joined me at the table I asked why he didn't introduce me. He told me that I looked ridiculous. **He was embarrassed of me.**

And guess what? The following weekend, the house in the Hamptons was full, so he couldn't bring me. Sorry!

I saw photos online. The girls from the previous weekend were invited. I was beside myself. What did I do wrong? Was I too young? Not serious enough? Not educated or traveled enough? Or was he only down for the fun and carefree part of dating me? Was I just not fancy enough for a *real* relationship?

There's another "don't."

**DON'T ever let someone make you feel less than.
It doesn't matter how old you are,
where you are from, where you went to school,
or how many stupid countries you've been to.
If they can't get with you for you, screw 'em.
Or wait, no—don't screw him, please.**

The next week, and for weeks to follow, I would barely hear from him. The texts went from few to none. After running into him at our shared favorite nightclub, he introduced me to his new girlfriend. An older, sophisticated English heiress. Well, he just said her name; I found the rest out through sleuthing. They were married later that year. I saw one of his kids on the subway once. And, yes, obviously I know what his kids look like **because I'm a very good stalker.**

I never did fully get over Brandon—still haven't. I think that's what happens with a slow fade. You're left with no closure, no ending. The slow fader leaves the impression he's keeping the door open so that he can come back through it at some point. You're left wondering why forever.

Don't give in to the slow fade. Don't run with it. Don't keep hoping it will reverse. **It won't; it's science!**

Another important "don't" in the slow fade phase is DON'T WAIT UP. I once "dated" this hunky strong silent type, Max. Just one of his thighs was as wide as me. He was a professional athlete, let's say football, who was incredibly regimented during game time but took full advantage of partying in the off-season. I was so desperately available, and desperate to see him, that I would wait up in bed in full makeup, sleeping on my back so as not to disturb anything. An outfit half on under my sheets. Weeknights, weekends, didn't matter. Some nights I would literally leave my house at 1 A.M. to meet him somewhere. **I would always hope he would get drunk and realize he missed me.** I wanted him to drunk text me. I'd put my ringer on high, juuuuuust in case I fell asleep. And, of course, vibrate—so there was no way I'd miss any opportunity.

And don't take this BS.

This is one of the biggest lines they feed us.

Ahem.

Yep.

I once met a guy outside a coffee shop who used the tiny bits of information he had—my first name and the college I attended—to find my Facebook profile and message me for my phone number. I'm telling you if they want it, they can make it happen.

So when your crush can't even
make time for a phone call at lunch,
run.

Maybe they don't slow fade. Maybe they just stop texting you completely out of nowhere. Fondly known now as "ghosting," my friends and I have another name for it, originating from this fun New Year's Eve tale.

I had met this guy, Sean, when he struck up a conversation with me while I was working at one of the Ralph Lauren stores on Madison Avenue. (I dressed the mannequins and set the window displays.) He asked my advice on which shirt he should buy to wear to this New Year's Eve party. I found him so charming. **We had great banter.** Then he asked if I was free to be his date. WOW! I had always wondered if this would ever happen to me at work.

We had a dreamlike New Year's Eve, a black tie party with champagne and confetti. Like the movies. We both had a couple of days off the following week for the holiday, and so he invited me to come to New Jersey with him to his grandparents' cabin. I met Grandma and Gramps. They were darling, hilarious. As it was full-on winter, we spent much of the weekend playing board games and drinking hot toddies, just the four of us by the fire. Can you picture it? Before we got on the road back to the city, Gramps pulled me aside. He softly whispered to me, "You're our favorite girl we've ever met." And then he kissed me on the cheek. My heart exploded. Was this a fricking Hallmark movie? Once back in the city, I sent thank-you flowers to Grandma, really trying to get those bonus points. I wrote Sean a jokey text asking if I had received those bonus points, and if Grandma had received her flowers.

Silence.

I went home to Allison that night. Our friend Matt came by, and we went over the weekend's events action by action, word for word together. They were searching for evidence that I had done something wrong, per usual. I kept reiterating that I was Gramps's favorite. Gramps caressed my forehead with his gosh darn blessing! Didn't that mean something?! Matt concluded that I had not been ghosted, but in fact I had been "nevsies-mindsies-ed." This meant he really did like me for a hot second, but then thought, *Actually, never mind!* We came up with a singsong chant to say "nev-sies-mind-sies" and a swinging hand motion. From that moment on, it was sort of a way to lift our spirits when any of the three of us got ghosted. So don't sink into an ice cream hole of depression if you're ghosted! Just laugh, shrug your shoulders, say, "welp," and sing, "nevsies-mindsies!"

I do still wonder if Grandma ever got her flowers.

A final "don't":
don't beat yourself up.

I was enamored with this guy, Luis, in college. He had sharp, beautiful blue eyes and perfect tan skin. He dressed like some man I imagined who lived in Paris or Milan, and who rode a motorcycle. Remember Paolo from the Lizzie McGuire movie? Like him grown up. I took him to sorority date parties, and we had long, amazing nights holding hands and walking the campus. But that was the problem. All we did was hold hands. And the occasional heavy make-out session. I seriously started to wonder what the heck was wrong with me. **Why didn't he want me?** I started to question everything about my-self. Was I not sexy enough? Was my personality meh, or did I smell? Most terrifying of all . . . was I just a bad kisser? Often I would worry that I'd ruined something by hooking up too soon. Now I was freaking out because we hadn't hooked up at all. Winter formals came around and Luis couldn't be my date because he was on the arm of someone else. A younger, prettier family friend of his named Jenny. Who he often told me "not to worry about" because she was "like his sister." Jenny had perfect skin, she was petite and brunette, giggly, with big boobs. They looked great together and, honestly, I couldn't compete. They were an instant item. Not the "sort-of" item we were. He started to keep me at a distance. Only group hangs. What had I done? What did she have that I didn't? We graduated and lost touch. I was crushed.

Years later, he moved to New York. He still had my number, and he reached out. We had dinner, and then I met his boyfriend. Luis is gay. And now he's one of my best friends. We laugh at the orange skin, overplucked eyebrows, and awkward make-outs from college. We're basically the modern-day Will and Grace. (But he's still never explained why he left me for Jenny.)

Okay, so even though I'm serving up some realness, claiming to be over everything, here's where I'm at most of the time.

Yes. Maybe once a day. Even now, **I think I'll be ninety-five and on my third husband, thinking about my ex from college.** I'd like to say it's normal. I think its BS when people think just because you're in a relationship, married, or have kids that the past is just erased. Who says you shouldn't still have feelings about what happened in your past? It's what made you. It's what led you to whoever you're with. There is nothing wrong with having a colorful romantic past—or present, for that matter. As I write this, I wonder if the guys I'm writing about will hear about this book. Will they read it? Will they reach out? Will they care? Was I just a blip for them, and would they be surprised that our three weeks to three months together impacted me so much?

At the end of the day, sadly, they probably
aren't thinking about you.

So go find someone who is.

Don't Go Back!

Just Don't

So, let's say you go to a restaurant. And the food is terrible. And the staff treats you like crap. Would you go back? Feck no. Well, then, why in the world do we go back to people who treat us like garbage??? WHY, I ASK YOU???

I had a man that I went back to over and over for seven years. I kid you not, people. It sounds insane, but I am not lying. Each time we were together, he would make some small reference to the future to keep me satiated. "One day when we're old and gray, ha ha ha . . ." And I'd think, *OMG, HE AGREES WE WILL EVENTUALLY END UP TOGETHER.* Just enough to leave me clinging to hope that one day . . . one day.

So, let's talk about this guy who led me on for three-quarters of a decade.

Let me begin by saying this story does not make me look great. In fact, I hesitate to tell it because it's kinda wrong. But I think more of us have done this—or considered it—than like to admit it.

His name was Leo, and he was Brandon's best friend. Yep. I went there. He was handsome and lanky, sort of a class clown. He had a dry sense of humor and loved to party. He made me feel good about being me. So, after Brandon's slow fade into oblivion, I found consolation in the arms of Leo one night. I think I was still grasping at a connection to Brandon, but also Leo was hot, and fun, and soooo . . .

We met up at a bar, and he told me he was sorry for the way I had been treated; **he thought I deserved better.** We kept drinking, we forgot about Brandon, and we decided to just have fun. After a night of tequila and dancing at 1 Oak, he ended up back at my place. He told me he had been the one who truly cared about me the whole time I was dating Brandon. He had feelings for me and hated watching Brandon ignore me. We didn't have sex, but it was close enough.

He woke up infuriated with himself for betraying Brandon. And I was a whirlwind of emotion. Why did I do that? Had I just lowered myself to this level, one I reviled—getting revenge on an ex by hooking up with his bestie? But wait, had Leo truly cared for me all along from the sidelines? Leo told me he felt too guilty and had to tell Brandon what happened. I begged him not to. Sent him novel-length reasons why he shouldn't via email.

Leo told Brandon, and their friendship was ruined for a while. Brandon told Leo he was never to see me again. Even after they mended their friendship, the ban was still on.

Well, we all know what happens with forbidden fruit.

That made us want each other more. We would meet up in secret. Late at night, or sometimes we would even escape together for a weekend. He would surprise me with a ticket to Vegas or something equally silly. I would ask him constantly, when can we actually stop this hiding and be together? Brandon was married by this point. Why would he even care?

There was always an excuse. Yet there would always be a next time. He would tell me we had a "special" relationship, unlike what he had with any other girl, and I believed it.

I became obsessed. I would come up with things to text him about. I would say I needed work advice or help fixing my air conditioner. Once I ordered a piece of IKEA furniture just to ask him to put it together.

Anything for an excuse to see him.

The sex was insane. I actually couldn't live without it. If Leo didn't reach out, I'd take it upon myself. Especially when out drinking. I wouldn't just double text him, I would bakers dozen text him. Then I would call if he didn't reply. And sometimes I would just show up at his door wasted if he didn't answer a call. You know, casual.

Sometimes we would spend nights on the couch at his place, cuddled up with takeout. We knew most everything about each other. It felt like what I heard about relationships. Minus the dates, romance, and commitment. Hm, looking back perhaps that should have been a clue? Every time I would allude to us taking the next steps, he'd brush it off and say, "Why ruin what we have now," or "Come on, you know it's not like that."

But wasn't it? Then why did we keep seeing each other? Why did we keep having sex? Why had he told me I was special and different from anyone else so many times? Why did he make vague references to the future? I know that I couldn't blame him for everything, as I was definitely complicit. I kept pushing back. I wouldn't accept his answers. But perhaps here's why; the kicker. During sex, Leo had told me he loved me. On multiple occasions. He used the words *I LOVE YOU*. I would bring it up as proof he cared for me, and he would simply attribute it to passion or heat of the moment. Can you imagine hearing "I love you" for the first time (repeatedly mind you) and then having it retracted, deemed meaningless? It would probably drive you to show up at someone's doorstep drunk, too. One day "it's not like that," the next night "I LOVE YOU."

I would write him emails and come up with grand plans: If by April 15 we still felt the same way, we would meet at X restaurant at Y time, and finally be a real couple. Sort of like Steve and Miranda at the Brooklyn Bridge. I bet these sad proposals are still in my Gmail.

So many of those dates and ultimatums came and went. I lost count of how many times I told him I was never speaking to him again.

I just kept reassuring myself that we kept meeting up
over all those years for a reason.

And what's worse, it would always distract me from anyone who was actually interested in me. I would be full-on seeing someone else, finally forgetting about Leo—and pop, here comes his text! I couldn't run fast enough to see him. And that would start the "maybe this time it's different" all over again. Hope would rekindle, and I would dump the new guy.

One night, after years of sex and confusion, in a drunken search for the truth, I texted him, "I just need you to tell me you and I will never EVER be together." And sure enough, he replied, "We will never be together in that way." I made a screenshot of it and kept it as my phone background for a while. Isn't that sick?

Sometimes you have to ask the hard questions.

The questions you don't ask because you already know the answer and don't want to hear it.

It's pretty crazy that it took me seven years to ask Leo directly if we would ever be a real couple. Pony up and ask a direct question, and you'll most likely get the direct truth.

Leo and I still text every now and then. We've somehow managed to stay friends. We can talk about the past and he often jokes asking if any of my drawings are inspired by him. (Many are.) He supports my art and he's happy for me. But I think there will always be a part of me that wonders if he ever actually cared. Or if secretly he still does. Was I actually special to him at any point?

The truth is, though, if he really wanted to be with me he could have and would have. And he didn't. Don't convince yourself otherwise like I did. Don't make excuses for them. Don't cling to a few words or small gestures with hope. You'll be waiting forever. I think everyone reading this probably has their own Leo.

Oof, let's lighten this up again, shall we?

Instead of going back to someone who hurts you constantly, choose pizza. It's just safer.

Don't give him things that he doesn't deserve anymore. Like your body, or even a sick poem. I think this may be one of my favorite things I've ever done. Once, after a particularly wild night at University of Michigan's Scorekeepers Bar & Grille, I wrote some verse for this dreamboat frat star I couldn't get over. (I've since tried to retrieve the email from the University of Michigan database, to no avail. Yes, I wrote this via school email.) It rhymed for a few paragraphs, if I remember correctly. I talked about football games and sorority names. Cheap beer and spreading cheer. You can laugh. The final line was something like, "A bond that will never sever, Arianna and Billy, friends forever." I thought the friendship angle could win him back.

Don't think that you can handle going back to him. You won't be chill. Don't think that you will be chill.

Once I tried to be chill. So chill it freezer-burned.

I was seeing this guy, Alex, long distance. We went on a couple of trips over the months in our respective cities, L.A. and New York. We said we weren't going to "define" anything, which I went along with, because what was the other option? Being an adult and saying I didn't want that? Pshh. I believed if I acted cool enough for long enough, he'd wanna actually date me.

We decided it would be fun to meet in Miami for a weekend. I got a spray tan. I worked out triple time, got a wax. I showed up with a suitcase full of outfits I had planned for weeks. He showed up with his best guy friend. The weekend was a total bust. Any time we weren't in our hotel room sleeping or having sex, we were with his buddy. I was trying so hard to be cool, but I just couldn't take it. When we both left for the airport, I thought we'd have one of those cinematic goodbye moments at the terminal. I tried to make it happen. I told him how much I cared about him. I didn't want this casual relationship, I wanted to be with him. I envisioned one of us moving. He told me he thought we were better off as friends.

I ASKED HIM, INFURIATED, WHY HE EVEN WANTED
TO GO ON THIS TRIP. WHY DRAG ME TO MIAMI?

**He told me he just wanted one more weekend
with me to be sure.**

To be sure it was over for him.

Well, I was glad I gave him the info he needed! I hated that answer. It was a knife in my stomach. Why was I always just the fun girl? **Why wasn't I one of those girls who people saw and thought, *That's a keeper.*** Then he left. My flight was delayed, so I went to this nautical-themed airport restaurant called the Islander Bar & Grill, got a table for one, ordered some fish and chips, and cried. Don't pretend you're down to just "have fun" if you can't.

Oh my lord, too depressing again? Well, if it makes you feel better, I often fly the same airline to Miami and visit the Islander (it's still there, Terminal D) and SMILE. Once I took a picture in front of it. Maybe I should start an emotional heartbreak sightseeing tour?

When I say, "don't go back to him," that also includes anyone close to him. Remember the Brandon and Leo saga? It never ends well for anyone involved. Don't mess with his friend group. It won't get his attention—at least not in a positive way. You may be thinking, "MUA-HAHA," but you will only make things worse.

I know there are feelings that remain even if you manage to keep from going back to someone. You still have all this anger building up inside, and so many words left unsaid. This book is probably proof that I'm full of that anger and those unsaid words.

But here's a pro tip—write them down. It feels so good to let it out. Don't give them more attention that they don't deserve. Remember Cooper? Meditation guy? Unfortunately, I didn't write down my thoughts. I just kept them bottled up inside until they exploded one night at Paul's Baby Grand at 3 A.M. It was a fashion week party, and I was in a room packed full of people when I saw him across the bar. I was a few margs deep. My friend Savannah literally had to hold me back with two arms as I screamed, "YOU MADE ME LOVE YOU!!!!" I'm not really sure what that even means, but apparently many people recall that I didn't stop repeating it.

Most important, if you're ever thinking of going back, please remember the biggest lie we tell ourselves of all time:

He's not.
And he never will be.

Boy Bye

You Didn't Really Like Them Anyway

Okay. Sometimes we can trick ourselves into liking someone because we just want to be in a relationship so badly. After we take a step back, did we really only like the idea of this person?

I was once bedazzled by a prince.

Yes, Prince Jonathan of . . . let's say Genovia, for privacy reasons. He was a real prince living in New York. In an uptown hotel nonetheless! Obviously, I would soon be an actual princess. ~pRiNcEsS~ had come a long way!

We met while I was on vacation with my parents in Florida. He took my number at some sceney watering hole in South Beach and said he'd call me when he got back to the city. I googled him, freaked out, and anxiously awaited his call. It actually came. Jonathan was always put together, his hair perfectly tame and his shirts perfectly pressed. His apartment was spotless because, well, it was in a hotel. The prince dined out every night, and I went with him. Steak houses, fancy Italian spots—I was his arm candy, and I liked it. He seemed to know everyone in New York. We went to charity events, galas, balls. He belonged to private clubs and social organizations. I remember fondly the first time he made me try escargot. My nose wrinkled. "Here, just drown it in butter and you'll love it." I thought to myself, *Wow, I wonder if this is what the rest of my life could be like.*

But there were other moments that made me wonder what my life would be like with him—in a different way. In the months we dated, we never kissed on the lips once. Not. Once. (To be perfectly clear, yes, we were sleeping together.) I felt like Pretty Woman, but only in the first part of the movie. I know what you're thinking: *How is that even possible? You're lying.* I wish I was. I would look less pathetic.

At first, I thought it was so weird that he would go directly to kissing my neck or boobs and then take off my clothes. Then I just kind of got used to it. We would fool around, kiss other places, have sex, but it never felt intimate—which I believe is what he wanted. **I never spoke up for fear that he would drop me.** I was sacrificing the chance of a tangible emotional connection for a title and what I thought would be a "relationship."

I wanted so bad for it to work. I wanted to force myself to be fine with it, but I wasn't. Luckily, one night I got too drunk and embarrassed him at a birthday party. Our romance ended with me screaming at him, slurring my words and barefoot on Fifth Avenue, holding my painful heels. I don't particularly remember exactly how the fight started, but I'm pretty sure it had something to do with me being too drunk. Which I indeed was. I let everything out. About the intimacy, my confusion, my desire for more. I was crying by the end, and I threw one of my shoes at him. Not really proper princess behavior, I suppose.

Are we all just too focused on this?

Or creating guidelines like this?

We have fairy-tale syndrome that teaches us at a young age there is someone perfect out there.

Sometimes our intuition tries to give our heart a clue. We begin to waver. His text comes in, and you put your phone back down. You can't decide if you should go out with him on Wednesday or not. You wonder what your friends are doing when you're with him. **He puts his arm around you, and you almost get annoyed.**

And then we try to change the person into someone we do like. That's a pretty clear sign.

There was one guy—oh, Henry. How I tried to force my heart to burn for him. We met through my cousin. Southern, football-player build. . . . He was the kind of guy who called his mom but would punch someone out at a bar for you. He was ambitious, a VP at a global media company and not yet thirty. Everyone wanted him around. He was confident, but not in a douchey way. I truly think if I said I wanted to get married, he would have the next day. He adored me, and I knew it. And I admit that I took full advantage.

Let's say Leo or any other guy disappointed me. I'd call up Henry, and there he would be. **He'd take me on some creative whirlwind date, and then I'd stare into his big brown eyes and feel scared.** I remember looking in the mirror once before meeting him and saying to myself, "What is wrong with you?! HE'S PERFECT—LIKE HIM!"

You aren't perfect. I'm not perfect. And neither are these people we build up "on paper."

What you need is the person whose imperfections fit your own.

The heart doesn't look at résumés. It just feels that perfectly imperfect fit.

Speaking of not being perfect, can I take a brief detour?

I've talked a lot about how I've been hurt. But if I'm honest (and if you are, too), there have been a few along the way (like Henry) that I have done horribly wrong, and it's important to acknowledge this.

There was one guy who gave me everything I'd thought I wanted, but I still ran.

It was December, a week until Christmas. I had been dating Carlos long distance for about a month. He was from my hometown, and he moved from New York back to Detroit after starting one of the first major humor Instagram accounts. He was kind, sensitive, and incredibly bright. He was an idea guy. We talked about world domination together—we'd start some sort of creative venture as a couple and travel, have some babies in Italy, a house in the French countryside, everything. I decided this was it. Exactly what I had been searching for all these years was here. I was going to move back to Detroit with him to start our life together. (Are you sensing a pattern in my hasty decision-making?)

It was all unicorns and rainbows until the move got closer. Carlos came to help me pack up, and I found myself getting annoyed with him. He'd ask how I was feeling, and I'd get frustrated. He'd move a box to the wrong place, and I'd scream at him. I didn't want to hug or kiss him. I wasn't excited at all, just nervous and scared. He left for the airport, and I felt relieved. I was going to meet him two days later in Detroit, on Christmas Eve.

I had quit my job, my apartment lease was up, and I was laying on a mattress awaiting my flight. My phone rang. I felt so alone in that empty, gray apartment, and the phone's ring seemed to echo forever. It was my father, God bless him. His super-low radio voice boomed. "You know, Arianna . . . you don't have to move." How did he know? I exhaled. It was as if someone had released me from my self-inflicted relationship prison. I was on track to move home, get married, have kids—everything was set. **Because it was what I thought I wanted. But I wasn't ready.**

I started crying. "I don't want to move, Dad."

Then he took a turn and exhaled. Because he knew he was going to have to be the one to help clean up the mess.

"Now hang up and see if you can get your job back!!! We'll figure out the rest later!"

I called Carlos on Christmas Eve and not only told him that I wasn't moving, but that I didn't want to be together at all. Merry Christmas. I puked afterward, disgusted with myself. And to make matters worse—I've never admitted this to anyone before—I flew to Mexico a couple of days later for another fling with Leo.

Another big "don't" is . . .

don't like someone for the wrong reasons.

You don't want to disappoint Chris Harrison. And it's not fair to them or to you. I made this mistake with a man who worked with a very famous pop star. To be fair, I was obsessed with him for all the right reasons at first—he was brilliant, artful, passionate, and kind. But then he dumped me. It was only when he asked me to take him back that I thought . . . *Weeellll, perhaps with this big fancy tour starting, my heart could find a way to repair itself?*

I went from city to city with him and the A-list posse that surrounded him, running around every night as his "assistant." I got tickets for all my friends, and we partied until the wee hours of the morning. I kept trying to get my scorched heart back to where it once was. *Just go with it*, I thought. Alas. All the backstage access in the world could not revive my feelings for him. On some level, I think he was probably using the fanfare to win me back as well. Fairly disappointed with my user self, I told him it had to end midway through the tour.

Okay, now let's get back to blaming other people, shall we?

LOL, JK. You see, it was never really about those other people. They were never even really ours . . .

So pour one out.

Because we never even really wanted them.

Focusing on You

I Mean,
You Get This One,
Right?

So, here's my biggest "don't."

Don't spend so much time worrying about what you mean to someone else. Don't worry about their approval or their opinion of your self-worth. And that applies to anything, not just romance.

IN THE WORDS OF MY QUEEN, RUPAUL,

"If you can't love yourself, how in the hell you gonna love somebody else?"

Let's focus on what we do have, and not what we don't. Do you have a cool job? Hobby? A talent? A telekinetic power? **Use it. Practice it. Own it.**

Heck, do you have a grudge? Or perhaps a hundred, like me? Let's turn it into a positive! Some will fight me on this, but I say a little revenge is great for some motivation. An evil coworker won't leave you alone? Work extra hard to be promoted above them so you don't have to deal. Your high school bully got featured in *Vogue*? Become an editor there so it won't happen again. Visit your ex's new restaurant. Not to eat but to ask how much it is to buy the building. Set some goals.

MONDAY

∘ SPIN CLASS
∘ DRINKS w/ REBECCA

TUESDAY

∘ YOGA
∘ WORLD DOMINATION
* DONT FORGET!

You'd be surprised how quickly you get over someone
when you start getting obsessed with yourself.

OH SNAP,
WE FLIPPED THE BUSY ON THEM!

I only recently became so enlightened, and I truly believe it's because I started to *WINCE* love myself.

OH BROTHER.

My art made me come alive.

It gave me purpose and passion. I stopped constantly thinking about when he was going to text me, and more about what my next creative endeavor was going to be. Then, as I was knee-deep in doodles, one of the dating apps finally led to something real. But I can't blame the apps for everything that had gone wrong in the past; it was me who was buggy.

**Once I exuded drive and excitement about life,
I met someone who was drawn to it.
I wasn't trying to lasso him with a wedding garter.
I told him I'm headed this way, and if he wanted to come
along, he'd better keep up.**

I don't want to preach to you or tell you there are some simple tools for success.

I don't have all the answers.
(CLEARLY.)

And to be honest, I'm sure I'll mess up again. Heck, I bet since I've written this book some drama/stupidity has unfolded. Relationships, marriages, families, they all hold new challenges, different issues to tackle. Meeting someone doesn't end with a perfect rainbow! Love is the most amazing feeling in the world, but it's riddled with complexity. Life happens. That perfect couple you see on Instagram? It's crap, sorry. What matters in the end is that you're happy with yourself, not yourself only if its contingent on someone else's approval.

But I want you to take a look at yourself. Have you done a self-inventory lately? Think back on the interactions you have. Have you taught someone something, have you made someone laugh, have you made someone feel safe?

Have you given someone a glimmer of hope or stood up for someone's rights? Have you contributed to a project at work, or is there a valuable service you provide every single day? What if you weren't there? Think of all the people you would affect. Think of how much the little things you do matter.

Now think about what you can do. I think we are pushed to work, work, work in life. It feels like you're going to look up years later and you're almost retiring. Is there something you've always wanted to do but made excuses not to? Whenever I'd complain to my parents about being too busy to start a passion project, they'd always tell me that there's no such thing as "not enough time." It's just like the guy who told you he's "too busy." Too busy is BS. **If you want something, you make the time.** Period. So start treating yourself better! Stop ignoring your own texts and ghosting your talents and capabilities! Ahh, sweet irony.

The internet is a crazy amazing place where you now theoretically have the ability to connect with anyone and everyone to help build your dream. You can DM Beyoncé. Make an Instagram for your love of cacti or create a blog about your favorite meal prep. Share tips on pet grooming. Traveling on the cheap. Or maybe you have a totally off-line passion. Start a book club. Design a dream clothing line. What is it that revs your engine? The minute you decide to get going on you is when you stop worrying about everyone else.

Did you learn some stuff? Did you think some thoughts? I want you guys to know that sometimes I wish I could go back and shake myself and tell myself to stop being such a doormat. But I'm also proud of my mistakes. While I probably cried enough tears into my pillow to fill seventy-seven venti Frapps, I'm grateful.

Because they made me realize what I DON'T want.

And what I DO need.

And what I DO deserve.

Acknowledgments

Acknowledging

THE MISTAKES

THE ANXIETIES

THE SUNRISES WHILST PARTYING

THE TEARS

THE NEGATIVE THOUGHTS

THE INSECURITIES

FOR PUSHING MY A$$ TO WORK HARDER

Mom, Pops, B, Blair, and Jilly,
for loving this weirdo.

My Rajko and Vesna

My friends,
for LOL-ing at me and with me.

Meg Thompson and Ashley Collom,
for building a dream.

Donna Loffredo,
for shaping the dream.

Vision LA—Meg, Nina, and Champs,
for believing the dream.

Instagram and the support of all the wonderful people online,
I'm proud to call you my friends even though we've never met.

About the Author

Arianna Margulis is currently navigating New York City by way of small-town Michigan. As a relationship-obsessed fashion girl, she began doodling about her day-to-day dramas on the floor of her studio apartment and decided to expose her innermost feelings to the world. Thus But Like Maybe, the girl cult Instagram, was born. From painting street-size murals and major brand collabs to enacting revenge on "ex-boyfriends," her imaginary best friend has created a world of opportunity she never thought possible. But most important of all, her drawings have brought her self-confidence, motivation, and love. Armed with a Sharpie and fueled by margaritas, she's ready to take on the world.